A

CHARADE,

OR

PARLOR DRAMA.

A Night with Charles XII. of Sweden,

OR,

A SOLDIER'S WIFE'S FIDELITY.

CHARACTERS.*

Charles XII., *King of Sweden.*

Major-General, Count **Sparre**,† Colonel of a Dragoon Regiment.

Captain-Lieutenant, Baron **Erick Sparre.**

Sergeant **Peter Larsen**, [(a Veteran of the Wars of CHARLES X. GUSTAVUS, and CHARLES XI.) belonging to the King's Grenadier Regiment, UPLANDIA,] attached as an Orderly to the King's person.

Baroness **Olga Sapieha**, wife of *Captain-Lieutenant* **Erick Sparre.**

Polish **Heiduc.**

---

*For Costume of **Charles** XII., see *Frontispiece* to Vol. I., "LEBEN **Karl** DES ZWOELFTEN KŒNIGS IN SCHWEDEN MIT MUNZEN & KUYPERN. **Johann Heinrich Weubel**, 1745"

For Costumes of *Major-General, Count* **Sparr**; *Captain-Lieutenant, Baron* **Erick Sparr**, and *Sergeant* **Larsen**, see Accessories to the above *Portrait* and *Military Costumes* page 197, Vol. II; — "BORLESUNGEN KRIEGSGESCHICHTE," by *Lieutenant-General* **Jules von Hardegg**, *Stuttgart, Berlag von Franz Rohler*. 1856.

For Costume of *Sergeant* **Larsen**, more particularly, compare Plate "*Musketiere*," Figures 1683 & 1710; and Plate "*Grenadiere*" Figure 1704; Plate "*Dragoner*." Figure 1688; and Plate "*Subaltern Officiere*" Figure 1711, in the "UNIFORMEN DES PREUSSISCHEN HEERES IN IHREN HAUPTVERANDERUNGEN BIS AUF DIE GEGENWART BEARBEITET—GEZEICHNET UND LITHOGRAPHIRT VON **Edmund Rabe** *L. Sachse & Co., Berlin*, 1846.

For Costume of Baroness **Olga Sparr**, and Polish HEIDUC, see Illustration to face page 339 of the GEOGRAPHIA UNIVERSALIS of HIERONYMUS DICELIUS, *Leipzig*, 1697; and Figure 3, Plate 10, Vol. I, ICONOGRAPHIC ENCYCLOPŒDIA; and Vol. III., page 167–339, *Text;* of same, likewise.

†SPARRE is spelled SPARR, (without the E,) in the THEATRUM EUROPŒUM.

SCENE I.

A mediæval Polish castle upon the *Bug*, in *Old Mazovia* (now *West Gallicia*). A gloomy chamber, scantily furnished, serving as the King's Quarters, dimly lighted by a single window looking out upon a wild, flat country, covered with snow. Sergeant LARSEN engaged in kindling a fire in a vast fire-place.

Enter King CHARLES, as if from a hard ride, his cloak and boots covered with mud. He throws off his cloak and heavy gloves, strides up to the fire, and seats himself in front of it upon a camp-stool. Sergeant withdraws and stands *"at Attention."*

KING. (*Warming his hands*)—Cold, Sergeant! (*abruptly.*)

SERGEANT. Bitter, bitter cold, Sire! The cursed wood is as obstinate and sappy as the Polish serfs who cut it.

KING. But, we Swedes don't mind the cold, eh, Sergeant?

SERGEANT. No! nor summer's heat either, Sire.

KING. True! The great GUSTAVUS taught us that. Ha! The *Kaiserlings* called him the Snow-King, who would melt as he advanced to the south; but HE melted the *Imperialists* with his new artillery.

SERGEANT. True, Sire! You are a Snow-King, too, for my first fight under you was a victory won in a snow storm.

KING. Where, Sergeant?

SERGEANT. At *Narva*, where we, 8,000 Swedes, beat 100,000 Russians in their entrenchments.*

---

* "King Charles, the conquering boy,
Stood up in dust and smoke;
He shook his sword for joy,
And through the battle broke.
How Swedish iron bites!
We will make trial new;
Stand back, ye Muscovites:
Forward! my own TRUE BLUE!

Not ten to one appal
The angry VASA'S Son;
Those fled, who did not fall:
So was his course begun.
He drove three Kings asunder,
Who leagued against him stood;
And Europe saw with wonder
A beardless Thunder-god."

CHARLES XII., on his Festival, 1818,
by ESAIAS TEGNER, Bishop of Wexio.

KING. True, Sergeant, we did it well. There were plenty to kill, plenty to be taken prisoners, and plenty to run away.

SERGEANT. I stood by when you said that, Sire!

KING. Ha! How so?

SERGEANT. It was when you told us we must trust to our bayonets; and, so we and the sleet charged right slap together in the Muscovites' faces.

KING. (*After a pause.*) Under whom did you first see fire?

SERGEANT. Under **Charles X. Gustavus**, Sire. He was a Snow-King, too. I beat the drum in Count NICHOLAS BRAHE's Upland regiment, when the King crossed the Belt upon the ice, and—

KING. (*Interrupting him.*) Wore a shirt over your uniform, to make you look like a moving snow-ball, when he besieged *Copenhagen* in mid-winter, and came near adding a fourth crown to the other three he heired from his lion fathers.

SERGEANT. He was a hero, indeed, Sire; and, under him, the Swedish lion came near eating up the Danish elephant.

KING. (*Musingly.*) Aye, by my three crowns! And he had a *hero* for a schoolmaster, gouty, stout, unconquerable **Torstenson**, under the Crown of Sweden, Sweden's greatest General in her greatest war. (*Starting up from his seat, and striding to and fro.*) He was a great man! How *he* made *his* artillery play! The Austrians nicknamed him "LIGHTNING." They might well, for he shattered them like that. (*Dashing a cup to pieces on the floor.*)

SERGEANT. Pottery 's scarce upon the *Bug*, Sire. You 've broken your last cup! (*Drums without, hurried steps, sounds of a guard falling in and presenting arms. Sergeant assumes a place in the back ground, and stands "at attention."*)

SENTRY (*without*). *Major-General, Count* SPARRE!

(*A knock at the door.*)

KING. (*Signals the Sergeant to admit whoever knocks.*)

Major-General, Count SPARRE *enters in a state of great agitation, and throws himself at the King's feet.*

GENERAL. Sire, mercy! Spare him, he is my only son!

KING. (*Coldly.*) Rise, General. (*Rising himself, and striding to and fro, speaking as if to himself.*) Just so! Men know their duty, and yet, to indulge a passing whim, peril an army. They have no mercy for their country, and yet they dare to ask their King for mercy for themselves. (*Abruptly.*) Sergeant! if a sentry sleeps upon or leaves his post, what says the law?

SERGEANT. Death, Sire!

KING. Even if he sleeps benumbed with cold?

SERGEANT. Death, Sire!

KING. Worn out with fatigue, he drops asleep!

SERGEANT. Death, Sire!

KING. What, no excuse?

SERGEANT. (*Astonished, and evidently not knowing what the King is driving at.*) Such excuses are all very fine, I know, Sire; but, of them, there is nothing said in the regulations.

KING. Death and the devil! Although fatigue or cold overpowers the poor soldier so that, despite himself, he sleeps upon his post, the officer will show no mercy to the private; shall I then pardon the officer who quits the position which his King assigned him to gratify a weak and nervous woman? No! By the three crowns which I bear upon my shield, your son, Count SPARRE, shall die. Has the Court Martial sat?

GENERAL. It has, Sire!

KING. And the sentence is——

GENERAL. Death within the next twenty-four hours after its confirmation by your Majesty.

KING. And that will be before I sleep.

GENERAL. (*Murmuring.*) Mercy, Sire!

KING. (*To Sergeant.*) Old Brahe musketeer, attention! (*The Sergeant brings his hand to the front of his grenadier cap, and stands at strictest attention throughout the rest of the scene*) Our troopers wanted forage, and I sent a cornet of the Polish horse to beat the country and bring in supplies. To cover their retreat in case they were attacked, I stationed Captain-Lieutenant, Baron SPARRE at Granna village. Three miles thence, his wife—what does a soldier with a wife?—lay sick; at all events, she said so; and this SPARRE, not hearing of the Poles, now due a day and more, leaves his command, and gallops to that wife. The *Major General* DOUGLAS,* in making the rounds of the outlying posts, finds a Command without its Commander, has him arrested, sends him before the Court Martial of his regiment, and he is tried. These are the facts, General, are they not?

GENERAL, (*Despondingly.*) His wife was dying, Sire!

KING. What say you, Sergeant, does a dying wife excuse a soldier? ah! I forgot, an officer, from his duty?

---

*There was a famous General of this name in the XXX Years' War. He was of Scotch descent, and besides otherwise distinguishing himself, inaugurated the charge of Cavalry "en muraille," at Jankovitz, a movement which decided that famous day.

Upon closer examination of authorities, it is more probable that it was Major General HAMILTON, who was present upon the occasion. He, also, was of Scotch descent, and commanded under CHARLES XII. in this campaign.

SERGEANT. A wife 's all very fine, Sire ! but there is nothing about one in the articles of war.

KING. Well, Sergeant, what does he merit ?

SERGEANT. Death !

KING. Major-General Count SPARRE, you have my answer by that old moustache. Retire ! Whatever the Court Martial has decided, I, CHARLES the King, confirm. (*Re-seats and covers himself.*)

(*Drums without, sounds of a guard falling in and presenting arms.*)

SENTRY. (*Without.*) Colonel, the Baron CRONHIELM !

KING. (*Significantly.*) The President of the Court Martial.

Major-General, Count SPARRE, *with a gesture of despair, retires as the door opens, and*

*THE SCENE CLOSES.**

SCENE II.

—Same as Scene I.—

KING **Charles** *discovered at a table covered with plans and despatches. The Baroness* SPARRE *rushes in* [through the door at the rear] *and throws herself at his feet.*

BARONESS. Sire ! spare my husband ! He is innocent ! I alone am guilty ! I deceived him—he was too faithful to disclose my fond deceit, and he will die without avowing it !

KING. (*Rising and retiring behind the table, which he keeps between him and the Baroness during the whole interview.*) Madam, the beauteous Countess KŒNIGSMARK—mark me !—the daughter of the Polish Ex-King, now, once more, the Saxon Elector, once waylaid and sought to move me with her tears.

BARONESS. (*Dejectedly*) Yes ! You turned your horse, and galloped off without a word.

KING. Apply the moral to yourself.

---

* As this CHARADE is intended for Representation in a Private House, and is particularly adapted to one having two Parlors, separated by folding doors, the Scenes are managed so that the folding doors can close or a curtain fall between the Scenes, in order to enable the Actors to place themselves, and arrange the accessories, without supervision and at their leisure.

† "Old grey-haired schemers muttered
Their plots with wily care ;
The brave young hero uttered
One word, and burst the snare.
High-bosomed, gold-haired, slender,
A new Aurora came :
From his Throne's young defender,
The temptress turned in shame.

ESAIAS TEGNER'S **Charles** XII.

Baroness. (*Imploringly.*) Are you that King who conquered Poland's kingdom only to give the crown away to a dear friend, and will you not receive a wife's, a mother's, prayer, who begs you but to hear her plea for one who is a crown to her, her husband ?

King. (*Calling.*) Sergeant!

Enter, Sergeant.

King. How comes this woman here ?

Sergeant. Sire, some secret passage brought her past the guard, and she presented me an order to admit her to your Majesty.

King. (*To Baroness.*) Who signed that pass ?

Baroness. The King of Poland.

King. Knows he the facts ?

Baroness. (*Confused and hesitating.*) He does, Sire !

King. Then I mistook the man. I thought he was a soldier. Sergeant, remove this lady. Look to it. As for to-night, no matter ; if we lie here to-morrow, see that all the castle walls are thoroughly examined for such clandestine passages. Charles of Sweden, with his sword, fears nothing, but a Swedish General must not be quartered where a spy can enter without challenge. Madam, a crime against the King, the King might pardon ; against the kingdom, never. No crime so grave as breach of discipline. The kingdom, the safety, and the honor of the Swedish realm, its glory, power, rests, sustains itself, but on the army. He who but weakens that support, even by the least infringement of the laws of war, is a worse traitor to the Swedish crown than the poor wretch who strikes at the King's life. The King is mortal, and must die, to-morrow or some day. The kingdom is immortal ; its soul 's the army. Who seeks to kill that soul, I say, must die. You hear me ?

Baroness. Alas ! too clearly. (*Swoons.*)

THE SCENE CLOSES.

SCENE III.

A vaulted underground and gloomy room in the same castle. No furniture except a rude settle and deal table. A rough bed upon the floor in one corner.

Captain-Lieutenant, Baron Sparre *discovered seated, sustaining the* Baroness *his wife, who has fallen across his knees. They are engaged in a conversation which has commenced before the scene opened.*

Baroness. Oh, my husband, I have murdered you. For one short hour of bliss after so many weary months of absence and of anxious terror, I must be without you now, until death only bring us to each other's arms again.

Baron. I blame you not, my Olga. Those who love pardon whate'er is done by their beloved ones, for the sake of love. I cannot understand it yet. How could you get that cursed order, which made me leave my post and seek you ?

Baroness. Alas ! alas ! When the King Leczinski was yet a simple Palatine and I a simple noble maiden, we were at school together, and it was oft remarked, our writing was so much alike that none conld tell the difference. Day by day I followed you in every movement of the Swedish army. A faithful servant advised me you were posted near my father's castle. Despairing lest the fate of war should drive you far from hence without an interview, heart-sick, half mad, I forged an order purporting to be the Polish King's, upon a scrap of paper on which your tyrant Charles had scrawled his name, which served as a countersign and his approval.

Baron. Tyrant, my wife ! He is my King, and just.

Baroness. Oh, husband, justice such as his is not the justice Heaven approves. Such iron justice makes the Swedish nation soldiers all. The sword they live by, and we read that those who live but by the sword shall die thereby. Oh, husband, and has it not slain you ?

(*As she ceases speaking, the sound of steps are heard, as it were, within the rear wall itself of the room, succeeded by a murmur of conversation, carried on in a low tone, stifled and rendered very indistinct by the intervening masonry. Silence. The Baroness steals towards the back of the stage, motioning the while her husband not to speak. Voices again.*)

Both together. (*In a whisper.*) Hark !

Baroness. (*After a short pause, during which the conversation is resumed.*) The words are Polish, and they seem to issue from the wall. (*Rushing and applying her ear to the wall, and listening intently.*) Oh, Erick ! They mention the King's name, and speak of death !

Baron. (*Rushing toward the wall, and then stopping midway precipitately.*) Curses upon it ! I cannot understand the Polish. Olga, listen. What do they say ?

Baroness. (*Listening with strained attention. Pause. Then returning to the front with an expression of intense anxiety, falling at her husband's feet, and clasping his knees.*) Husband, in case of the King's death, who next succeeds to the command upon the *Bug ?*

Baron. Why ask you ? Heavens ! The General Steinbock.

Baroness. And he is your mother's brother. Doubtless he would respite ; perhaps, knew he the truth, would pardon you.

Baron. Olga, are you mad ? (*Solemnly.*) I am about to die. I charge you, if you love me, tell me, what have you heard ? Explain this mystery.

Baroness. Dearest husband, it was noised abroad that if the Swedish King should die by violence, the Cardinal Primate* would absolve the criminal who slew a heretic, persecutor of the true Romish Church. From the words I heard just now, the King of Sweden's life is in danger. I heard the King Augustus named. Reward! Kill! Heretic-King! Those words were spoken in a secret passage, of which so many pierce these castle walls. The one in which we heard that conversation, leads into the chamber where the Swedish King is sleeping, far from his guards, his staff; his only sentinel an old and war-worn Sergeant.—

Baron. Oh, misery! And I, a prisoner, cannot warn, protect him! Ho! without there!

Baroness. (*Stopping his mouth with her hand.*) Unheard, refusing to hear me, he has condemned you.

Baron. He is just. He is my King. (*He is about to rush to the door, and endeavor to arouse the guard,*)

Baroness. (*Clinging to him.*) Stay, hear me, husband, hear me. You will not be listened to. Before the guard can be aroused whoever is in the secret passage can gain the King's apartment. Scarce an half-hour since, I made my way into the King's own antechamber by another shorter passage through the wall. He gave orders to-morrow morning,—not before,—to have the walls examined. By that passage I can make my way far quicker to the King than those we have heard. [(*Aside.*) A hope inspires me.] (*Aloud.*) Husband, I can, I will preserve him!

Baron. (*Solemnly.*) Olga, can I trust you?

Baroness. Erick, it was I that caused your peril, cast a stain upon your honor. By thy true heart, I will preserve that honor now, and save the King. (*Rushes to the door, and knocks violently.*)

Sentry. (*Without.*) Ho! Who knocks within there?

Baroness. 'Tis I! The prisoner's wife. Quick! Open to me. You have seen my pass.

Sentry. (*Without.*) Yes; I know it! Quick! Come out! The night wears fast.

(*Door partially opened. The Baroness rushes out.*)

Baron. (*Solus. After a pause, and reflection.*) That I love her so well, makes me distrust her present purpose. Hoping that the King's death may save my life, she may delay, and Charles be murdered. Better a million, such as I should die, than one such hero-King as he. (*Rushing to the door, shaking it violently, and knocking furiously.*) Ho! guard, without there!

---

*The Cardinal Primate of Poland, at this epoch, was Michael Radzieiowski, *Archbishop af Gnesne*, elevated to that dignity, September 2d, 1686.

SENTRY. (*Without. Rattling his musket as he brings it to a charge.*) Prisoner, be quiet. Retire from the door.

BARON. (*Imploringly.*) Soldier! The King's life is in danger. Fly! Alarm the guard.

SENTRY. (*Without.*) Thunder! And leave my post?—Retire from the door!

BARON. Sentry, are you a Swede?

SENTRY. I am, a faithful one; a Smaland man.

BARON. By Heavens! I swear, my, your, King's life 's in danger. Fly! Alarm the guard.

SENTRY. (*Without.*) A foolish fetch. Do you not know that he who quits his post dies by the letter of the law, when you have been condemned for quitting yours? Far distant, and above us, is the guard-room. A musket shot could scarce be heard there. Retire from the door, or I will fire upon you through the panel.

BARON. (*In despair, falling upon his settle.*) Heaven protect my King! I would, but cannot!

THE SCENE CLOSES.

SCENE IV.

Same as Scenes I. and II. Time, near midnight.

A candelabra standing upon the table, with the lights flickering in the sockets. The King asleep in a chair; a map lying across his knees, as if it had fallen from his hands while under examination. A slight but distinct noise is heard, just after the scene has opened, at one side, like the sound of a bolt carefully withdrawn from its socket. Pause.

The BARONESS *rushes into the room, and throws herself at the King's feet.*

BARONESS. [*With a cry of delight.*] In time! [*The King starts up, and throws her from him, and half-draws his sword, but, recognizing the* BARONESS, *thrusts it back with a contemptuous snap into the scabbard.*]

KING. [*Coldly*] Pshaw! Again, that woman! How dared you make your way, again, into my presence?

BARONESS. [*Pointing to one side of the apartment.*] By the secret passage, [*clinging to him,*] I come to save your life. Oh, spare my husband's!

KING. [*Striving to disengage himself from her, and speaking in a cold tone of voice.*] I answered you some hours since.

[*While this is occurring, a panel in the side of the apartment* BEHIND THE KING, *opens suddenly, and a person, dressed as a Polish* HEIDUC, *suddenly appears, and presents a pistol at the* KING, *whose back is turned towards him.*]

HEIDUC. Die, heretic and scourge of Poland!

BARONESS. [*By a violent effort interposing herself between the* KING *and the* HEIDUC, *just as the pistol is presented, and uttering a shriek of despair.*] Villain! you only shoot the King through me.

HEIDUC *fires and disappears;* BARONESS *falls.* KING *draws his sword, and rushes to the panel, to find it shut and bolted from without. Musket shots without, at different distances. A pause and silence; then sounds of galloping horse heard in the distance.*

SENTRIES. [*Without, challenging at different posts, more and more removed from the scene.*] Alert! To arms!

SERGEANT. [*Rushing in as the shot is fired.*] Thunder! The King! Guards! To us! To arms!

KING. [*Calmly.*] Sergeant, for an old soldier, you keep but slack watch. Lift up the Baroness—gently—she has saved my life.

[*Noise of feet heard without, and rapidly approaching. Soldiers heard rushing from different posts towards the King's chamber.*]

KING. [*Striding to the door, and turning the key.*] Ho, there without! Halt! —Order arms!

[*Sound without, of muskets brought to the Order.*]

SERGEANT. [*Who has raised the Baroness, placed her in the King's chair, and has been examining her dress.*] A miracle, Sire! [*Showing a locket.*] A pistol ball, which struck her in the breast, was turned aside by this gold ornament.*

KING. [*For the first time with feeling.*] Thank Heaven!

BARONESS. [*Faintly and slowly recovering from the shock*] Sire, spare my husband!

KING. Poor, faithful woman! Sergeant, what say you?

SERGEANT. [*With great simplicity.*] This is all very fine, Sire; but there is nothing about it in the regulations.

[*A knocking at the door.*]

KING. Who knocks.

GENERAL. [*Without.*] Major-General, the Count SPARRE!

---

*The great-uncle of the author, an officer in the British service, second in command at the battle of King's Mountain, in 1780, had his life preserved by a similar interposition. Conspicuous for his bravery and success, wherever present with his regulars, he was the special mark of the opposing riflemen, one of whose balls took effect in his side, but providentially stuck a gold doubloon in his pocket. The shock only threw him down but nevertheless determined the fate of the day. The doubloon, up to within a few years, was still in the possession of a member of the family.

KING. Sergeant, admit him—but alone—and stand aside.

GENERAL. (*Rushing in as soon as the door is opened, and stopping suddenly at a signal made by a wave of the King's hand*] Gracious Heavens! Your Majesty! Treason!—Two Polish Heiducs prisoners! Four shot! A squadron of dragoons sent in pursuit——

KING. Enough! I know it all. [*Stepping to the table, and hastily writing an order.*] Sergeant, take this order! Conduct hither, and without a guard, the prisoner, Captain-Lieutenant SPARRE. [*Exit, Sergeant.*]

BARONESS. [*At first speaking faintly, but gaining strength as she proceeds.*] Sire, hear me? You owe your life more to my husband than to me. I hoped that, if your Majesty should die, the General, your successor in command, would have had mercy on my ERICK. But my husband adjured me, by my love to him, to fly and save you without thought of self. He said that you were just; that he deserved his sentence; that to Sweden, your life was worth an army's. [*With great emphasis.*] IF you are that *brave, just* CHARLES,* your soldiers sing of, you can appreciate that soldier's love, who, when condemned to death, thought nothing of himself; thought only of his Monarch's safety.

KING. Lady, you know I am no lady's man, and little care for woman's tears or smiles; but when I witness truth in that vain, fickle sex, whose wiles my very soul abhors, I honor it as high as though a hero's heart beat 'neath the woman's boddice. GUSTAVUS VASA, he who laid deep and sure the corner-stone of Sweden's royal line, instituted the order of the SWORD, to recompense his soldiers' valor, truth and patriotism. I never heard a woman wore its Cross till now; but— [*disengaging a military decoration from the breast of his coat, and attaching it to the boddice of the Baroness*]—you shall be the first. And, by my crown, I pledge myself to grant your first request.

BARONESS. [*Instantly.*] My husband's pardon!

KING. That was granted ere you spoke.

BARONESS. Then I am satisfied. I have no more to ask.

KING. And now I must be just. Living to you, your husband's dead to me. He leaves the army. The officer who quits his post, as Captain-Lieutenant SPARRE did, can no more serve King CHARLES, the XIIth, of Sweden. Home, to Sweden, must he go forthwith, bearing with him earth's best and rarest treasure—a good and faithful wife. [*A knock at the door.*] Enter!

[*Enter,* SERGEANT *and Captain-Lieutenant Baron* SPARRE. *They halt in the back ground.*]

KING. Sergeant! What 's due that soldier who, by sacrifice of self, preserves his sovereign's life?

---

*"So great a heart was heaving
  In his true Swedish breast,
In gladness, or in grieving,
  JUSTICE *he loved the best.*
Though fortune smiled or lowered,
  He dauntless kept the field:
He could not be o'erpowered,
  He knew not how to yield."

ESAIAS TEGNER'S Charles XII.

SERGEANT. Nothing, Sire! It is his duty. What Swedish soldier would not die, Sire, a dozen deaths, to save you?

KING. Baroness, you hear! He speaks no more than truth, and Sweden's sons have proved it upon a thousand battle-fields. Captain-Lieutenant SPARRE, to the front! As a soldier-King, I cannot act but as a soldier should. I pardon you—

BARON SPARRE. Sire!

KING. [*Imposing silence by a gesture.*] Thank me when you know all. Lady, to me your husband's sentence would be harder to be borne than to be shot to death by a platoon of grizzly true-blue Upland musketeers, like yonder grim one. [*Pointing to the* SERGEANT.] But let that pass. You do not think so. You leave your fertile, wheat-producing plains for a rude land, which bears no crop but iron. [*To Captain-Lieutenant, Baron* SPARRE, *who makes a gesture of mingled astonishment and grief, but is restrained from speaking by the King's gesture*] I must make good the loss by the exchange. You shall be CHARLES' Superintendent of the Dalecarlian iron mines, with all the revenues of that important office. [*To the Baroness.*] Your husband can discharge the duty, but your's must be the honor [*motions the Baron and Baroness to approach him, takes their hands and joins them.*] Be prosperous and happy. With wealth and opportunities of doing good and serving Sweden's crown, I recompense a SOLDIER'S WIFE'S FIDELITY. What say you, Sergeant?

SERGEANT: It is all very fine, Sire! But I can't understand it, for there is nothing about it in the regulations.

ARRANGEMENT OF THE CHARACTERS,

King CHARLES,

BARONESS, BARON SPARRE,

Major-General Count SPARRE, Sergeant LARSEN,

AS THE

CURTAIN FALLS.

www.ingramcontent.com/pod-product-compliance
Lightning Source LLC
LaVergne TN
LVHW020638110826
845149LV00004B/1265

9781418189730